# Cottage Gardens

## Contents

2  Introduction

3  Working with bonding web

4  Scribble-quilting/doodling
   Before you begin …

5  Small Cottage Garden

8  Tall Cottage Garden

10  'Sissinghurst' White Garden

12  Show-Stopper Garden

15  Templates

Teamwork
CRAFTBOOKS

# Introduction

Flowers and gardens have inspired craftspeople since the earliest days, and I'm no exception. In contrast to many other quilters, the gardening gene has passed me by, but my husband Chris and I love looking at and enjoying the results of other people's green fingers – and I particularly enjoy cottage gardens. For me, nothing beats a gorgeous garden crammed with a riot of bright blooms in all shapes and sizes – the greater the variety, the better.

I felt that it was high time to immortalise a collection of cottage gardens in fabric and thread – probably the closest I'll get to creating a really beautiful garden! In these quilts I've tried to capture that fabulous riot of colours and textures, with lots of classic cottage garden favourites such as hollyhocks, foxgloves, daisies, poppies, delphiniums, marigolds, lavender, pinks …

A few years ago we visited Sissinghurst for the first time, and were very taken with its famous White Garden – so I've even included a Sissinghurst design, using white/cream versions of the classic blooms. Choose your favourite blossoms, and combine them as you wish: as with the gardens themselves, there's no right or wrong – the only limit is your imagination. Have fun.

Many of these flower motifs also work well for smaller projects: table-mats, a Kindle ™ cover, photo album, shoulder bag etc. And you can add even more variation by embellishing the designs with hand or machine embroidery and/or beads and charms. The examples here show how different the same basic design can look, depending on the fabrics you use for the motifs and background; I've also flipped one of the samples left-to-right, and added an extra leaf to another.

When you're choosing the fabrics for your flowers and foliage, make sure that they all show up well against your chosen background. Use plenty of variety, too, especially of tones and shades of greens for the stems and leaves; these will look really good when different stems overlap. Batiks work well for the motifs, as they are closely woven and also look naturalistic; marbled and shaded fabrics are effective too.

## Working with bonding web

We modern-day stitchers have all kinds of wonderful things available to us, and one of the very best is: double-sided bonding web. All the designs in this booklet are created by fusing the motifs onto the background with bonding web, then using my 'scribble-quilting' technique to produce a subtle stained-glass effect round the patches.

There are various types of bonding web available, but they all work in a similar way, allowing you to bond one piece of fabric to another pretty permanently. The ones I like best are Bondaweb ™ and Steam-a-Seam ™; Steam-a-Seam has the extra benefit that you can finger-press the patches in position before you fuse them permanently. Of course we are stitchers, not gluers, and all these projects are also quilted; on page 4 you'll find details of how to do my 'scribble-quilting' technique.

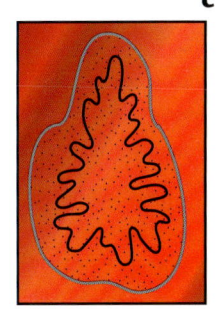
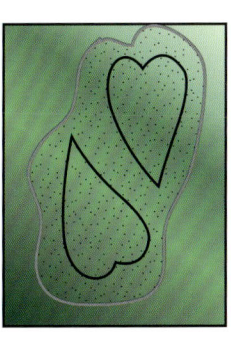
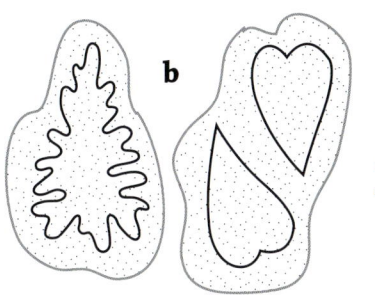
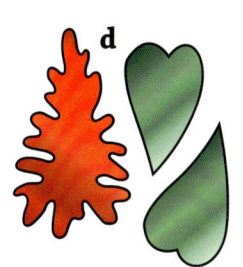
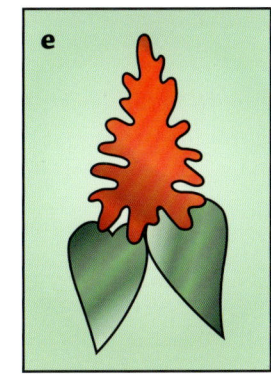

The basic method for working with bonding web follows these steps:

1. Using ordinary pencil, and working on the smooth (non-glue) side of the bonding web, trace your chosen shapes (**a**). If you're using lots of different flowers and leaves, write the name on each one to remind you which is which when you're assembling the design.

2. Cut the shapes out roughly, leaving a margin of bonding web outside each drawn line (**b**); this helps you to get a really good seal when you fuse the shape onto the fabric. If you are using one fabric for several shapes, you can cut the shapes out as a group rather than individually – again, just ensure that there is a margin of bonding web round each group.

3. Position the paper shape, glue side down, on the back of your chosen fabric (**c**); make sure that the fabric patch is slightly larger all round than the bonding web shape. (This will help you keep your ironing board free of sticky areas!)

4. Lay a greaseproof/non-stick sheet over the work, and use a hot iron to fuse the shape firmly to the fabric. If you're using Bondaweb, the paper will go slightly translucent, instead of white; that's how you know you've got a good seal between the layers. The bonding web manufacturers differ on whether the suggest steam or not; I've found that it doesn't seem to make too much difference. Cut the shape out along the marked line (**d**).

5. Once you're ready to fuse the shape into position on another fabric, peel off the backing paper. Position the shape, glue side down, on the right side of the background fabric (**e**); cover with the greaseproof/non-stick sheet, and iron the patch in place.

### Tips for working with bonding web

❀ When you can, use tightly-woven fabrics such as batiks; these will help you to keep really sharp outlines on the patches

❀ Always use a non-stick ironing sheet or greaseproof paper/baking parchment to protect the iron and board from stray stickiness …

❀ Remember that the bonding web always goes on the back of the fabric, glue side against the fabric

❀ Steam-a-Seam has paper on both sides of the glue web to protect it. When you've traced shapes onto one side, and want to peel off the backing paper, make sure that the glue web stays attached to the traced side!

❀ When you come to remove the backing papers from the fused shapes, scratch the paper with a pin; this makes it much easier to peel the paper off

## Scribble-quilting/doodling

This technique combines fusing with free machine quilting, working in dark thread to create a subtle stained glass effect. If you're new to free machine quilting, this technique is the perfect place to start, because (to be quite honest) it doesn't really matter where the lines go! The trick is to work several random lines of free machining round the edge of each shape, allowing each stitching line to meander between the appliqué patch and the background. It's as easy as doodling.

To do this technique, you need to set your sewing machine up for free quilting. Machines vary enormously in exactly how this is done – consult your manual for the details – but generally you need to do two things: attach a free machining foot (which is usually an open or closed ring of metal or plastic); and drop or cover the feed dogs – the little teeth that normally pull the fabric under the machine foot evenly. You can then move the fabric in any direction, which allows you to follow the shapes of the motifs really easily.

Once your motif is fused onto the background, and you've layered up your quilt with the wadding and backing (**a**), choose a place to begin stitching. Before you start, bring the bobbin thread up to the surface of the work, so that it won't get tangled up at the back of the work. Begin with lines that, visually, go into/underneath other lines – so, on this example, I'm beginning with the foliage at the top, and the leaves, both of which go behind the flowers (**b**).

Carry on building up the design in the same way until all the raw edges are covered with lines of scribble-stitching (**c** and **d**). Use at least three lines of stitching each time, so that you create a definite outline; if you want a stronger effect from the stitching, use four or five lines.

## Before you begin …

I've done several basic designs using different combinations of flower motifs, and on the following pages I'll talk you through how to put them together, but you will think of lots of other ways of combining and embellishing the designs. And, of course, you can also enlarge the shapes and use them in different ways – for instance, individual flowers edged with satin stitch or blanket stitch would look really striking worked on blocks and built into a large quilt.

### Whichever design you're doing, you will need:

- machine-quilting thread in a colour that contrasts well with your chosen fabrics (eg black, navy, dark green, dark purple, dark brown, or even white)
- sewing thread to match any borders, binding or cushion backings
- pencil
- non-stick ironing sheet or greaseproof paper/baking parchment; use this to protect the iron and ironing board whenever you're working with the bonding web
- small, sharp-pointed scissors – these are important: if yours aren't sharp right to the tip, now's the time to invest in some new ones!
- Frixion pen™ or chalk marker that will show on your fabrics, for drawing on extra details such as leaf veins
- rotary cutter, ruler and board
- optional embellishments: beads, charms, jewels, buttons, foils etc

# Small Cottage Garden

If you're new to working with bonding web, or to my 'scribble' technique, this is a perfect design to begin with. The shapes are striking, but relatively simple – and as you can see from the variations on pages 2 and 7, there are lots of ways in which you can vary the flowers. For instance, you could create the daisies in classic white with yellow centres, or bright yellow with dark brown centres (like black-eyed susans) – or you could make them look like Michaelmas daisies, with mauve petals and golden-orange centres, or even marigolds. And of course you can use some of the other smaller blossoms from the templates on pages 15-24, either as well as or instead of the ones I've used.

*My example is 15in (38cm) square, but you can make it wider or deeper if you wish; just alter the dimensions of the background, wadding and backing accordingly (the backing fabric and wadding should be about 2in/5cm larger than the background), and the length of the binding strip.*

**As well as the items on page 4, you will also need:**

- background fabric 15in (38cm) square
- large scraps of cotton fabrics in a mixture of colours and tones that work well against your background; bright colours (or white/cream) for the flowers, and a good selection of greens for the stems and leaves
- backing fabric, 17in (45cm) square
- 2yd (2m) binding strip that complements or contrasts with your background fabric; I used a single binding cut 2in (5cm) wide
- 20in (50cm) double-sided bonding web, 18in (45cm) wide; if you are creating a larger design, you will need more bonding web
- flat wadding, 17in (45cm) square

## Instructions

1  From the templates on pages 15-24, choose the plants that you would like to feature on your design; most plants will have foliage, and one or more flowers. (For instance, each California poppy plant has one flower; each daisy plant has three stems, and therefore three flowers.) There are also a few solo flowers (for instance the pinks, vincas, extra daises etc) which are good for filling in gaps.

Use pencil to trace the solid lines of the chosen shapes onto the smooth side of the bonding web (ignore any dotted lines at this stage). The arrows on some of the stems show that you can either shorten or extend them if you wish, to alter the heights of the plants in your garden. If you are using the same fabric for several shapes (for instance, for four or five lavender flowers), group these close to each other on the bonding web, then leave a small gap between that group of shapes and the next (**a**). Write the name on each shape to remind you what's what.

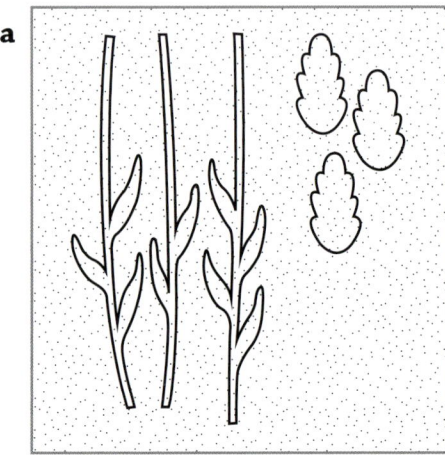

2  Cut all the shapes out roughly in their groups, leaving a border of bonding web around the pencil lines (**b**). Lay each bonding web piece, glue side down, onto the wrong side of the relevant fabric and fuse it in place with a warm iron; always use the non-stick or protective sheet between the work and the iron when you're fusing. Once everything is fused in place (**c**), carefully cut out all the designs along the marked pencil lines (**d**).

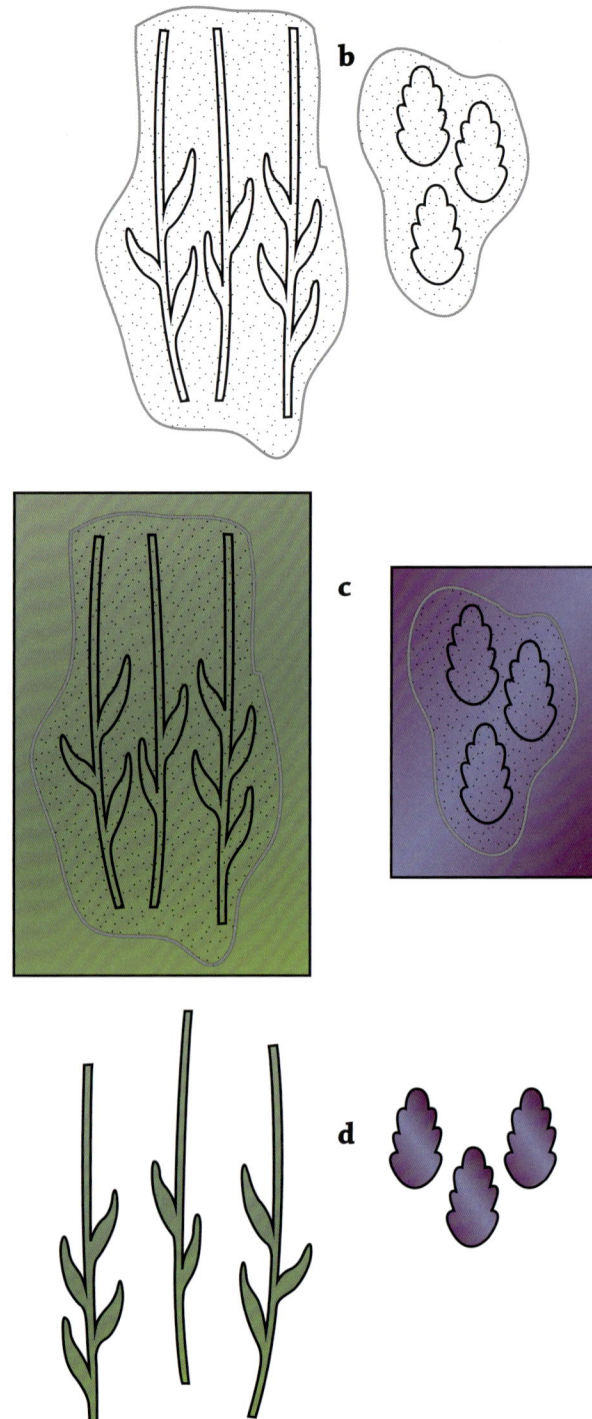

3  Peel the papers off the shapes; with each one, scratch the paper with a pin – this makes it much easier to peel the paper off. Lay all the shapes right side up on the background square, overlapping

them as much as you wish; take time to get an arrangement that works really well. If you wish, you can take all or some of the stems right down to the bottom of the square, but keep the motifs at least ½in (roughly 1cm) in from the other edges so that they don't get caught under the binding. Once you're happy with the arrangement, put in a few pins to hold the motifs in place; lay the non-stick sheet or paper over the top, and lightly fuse the shapes in position, then remove the pins and fuse them firmly (**e**).

4  Use a Frixion pen or chalk marker to draw in any extra (dotted) lines that were marked on the templates (for instance, the internal lines on the daisy flowers). Lay the backing fabric right side down on a flat surface and position the wadding on top;  lay the fused design, right side up, on top so that there's an even border of wadding all the way around the edge of the design. Use your preferred method to secure the layers. Follow the principles on page 4 to 'doodle' round the edges of the shapes (**f**), beginning with any shapes that go into or behind other shapes.

5  Use a rotary cutter, ruler and board to trim the quilt down to an accurate square, and use the binding strip to add a continuous binding around the raw edges. Add any embellishments (buttons, beads, charms etc) you wish. To hang the quilt, add a hidden casing at the top of the quilt on the back, or stitch on hanging loops of ribbon or tape.

*Below I've created two variations of the* Small Cottage Garden. *For the one on the left I used flame-coloured blooms on a lime green background, and bound it in citrus colours; for the cushion-cover on the right I used just poppy flowers and foliage, and added narrow and wider border strips before completing the cover.*

# Tall Cottage Garden

Foxgloves, hollyhocks and delphiniums are the stars of this quilt – three of the tallest members of the cottage garden population! All these three flowers come in a wide variety of colour variations (see page 10 too), and they are all created using two fabrics – one for the flower outsides, and one for the centres/insides. Build up a garden like mine, or mix and match these blossoms with the others from the template pages.

*Finished size: my example is 24 x 20in (60 x 50cm). You need a depth of at least 24in (60cm) in order to fit in the tall flowers, but you can make your version wider, narrower or deeper if you wish; just alter the dimensions of the background, wadding and backing accordingly (the backing fabric and wadding should be about 2in/5cm larger than the background), and the length of the binding strip.*

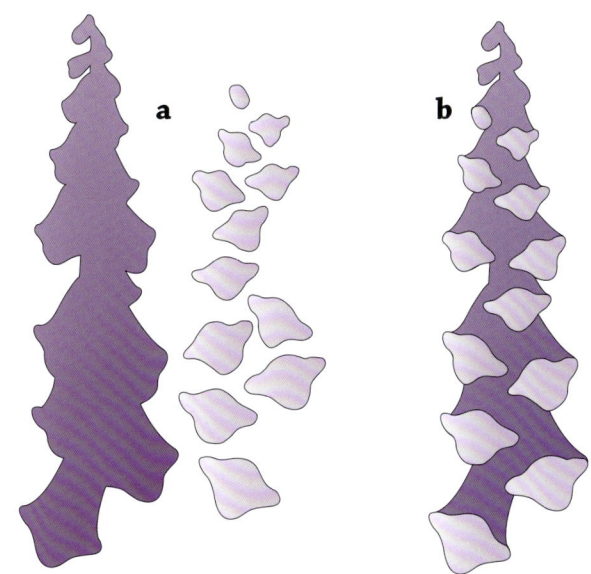

**As well as the items on page 4, you will also need:**
- background fabric 24 x 20in (60 x 50cm)
- large scraps of cotton fabrics in a mixture of colours and tones that work well against your background; bright colours (or white/cream) for the flowers, and a good selection of greens for the stems and leaves
- backing fabric, 26 x 22in (66 x 56cm)
- 3yd (3m) binding strip that complements or contrasts with your background fabric; I used a single binding cut 2in (5cm) wide
- 1yd (1m) double-sided bonding web, 18in (45cm) wide; if you are creating a larger design, you will need more bonding web
- flat wadding, 26 x 22in (66 x 56cm)

## Instructions

1. Using the templates on pages 15-24, trace the solid lines of the chosen shapes onto the smooth side of the bonding web (ignore any dotted lines at this stage). The arrows on some of the stems show that you can either shorten or extend them if you wish. Write the name on each shape to remind you what's what. Trace the flower centres in a separate group.

2. Follow the method on page 3 to fuse all the shapes onto the relevant fabrics and to cut out the shapes. If you're creating a composite flower such as a foxglove, hollyhock or delphinium, peel the papers off the centre shapes, but not the main background flower (**a**). Following the guidelines on the template, position the centres on the corresponding flowers – remember that the template is reversed left to right. Once you're happy with the positioning, fuse the centres in place (**b**).

3. When you've assembled any composite flowers, peel the papers off all the remaining shapes and follow the steps on page 7 to build up your design. Mark any extra (dotted) lines from the templates (some of these you can just stitch by eye), and layer the quilt with the backing and wadding. Follow the tips on page 4 to 'doodle' round the motifs (**c**).

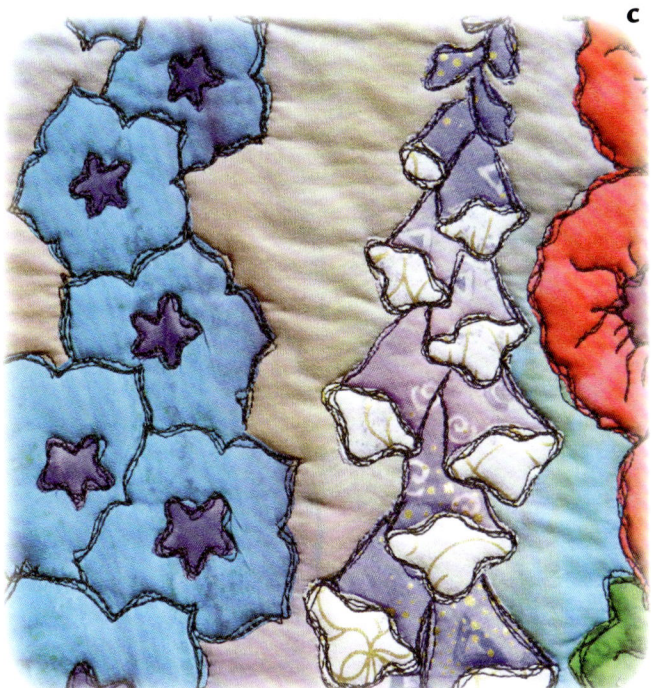

4. Use a rotary cutter, ruler and board to trim the quilt down to an accurate rectangle, and use the binding strip to add a continuous binding around the raw edges. Add any embellishments (buttons, beads, charms etc) you wish. To hang the quilt, add a hidden casing at the top of the quilt on the back, or stitch on hanging loops of ribbon or tape.

# 'Sissinghurst' White Garden

For my Sissinghurst-style 'white' garden, I've created lots of different flowers in shades of cream and pale green as well as white – and the different greens of the foliage add extra interest. I couldn't resist, too, adding lots of bead embellishments, but you can omit these if you prefer a plainer garden.

*Finished size: my example is 24 x 20in (60 x 50cm). As with the tall cottage garden, you need a depth of at least 24in (60cm) if you're going to use hollyhocks, foxgloves or delphiniums, but again you can alter the dimensions of the quilt as much as you like – just alter the wadding and backing accordingly (the backing fabric and wadding should be about 2in/5cm larger than the background), and the length of the binding strip.*

As well as the items on page 4, you will also need:

- background fabric 24 x 20in (60 x 50cm)
- large scraps of cotton fabrics in a mixture of whites, creams and very pale greens for the flowers, and a good selection of greens for the stems and leaves
- backing fabric, 26 x 22in (66 x 56cm)
- 3yd (3m) binding strip that complements or contrasts with your background fabric; I used a single binding cut 2in (5cm) wide
- 1yd (1m) double-sided bonding web, 18in (45cm) wide; if you are creating a larger design, you will need more bonding web
- flat wadding, 26 x 22in (66 x 56cm)

## Instructions

1. From the templates on pages 15-24, choose the plants that you would like to feature on your design. Follow the steps on pages 3 and 9 to trace, fuse and cut out the flowers, and to assemble any hollyhocks, delphiniums or foxgloves. If you'd like to include alliums in your design, draw 2½in (6.5cm) or 3½in (9cm) circles on the bonding web; fuse the circles onto the relevant fabrics, and then wiggle the scissors as you cut them out to create uneven edges (**a**). Create allium stems by cutting fine strips from green fabric backed with bonding web.

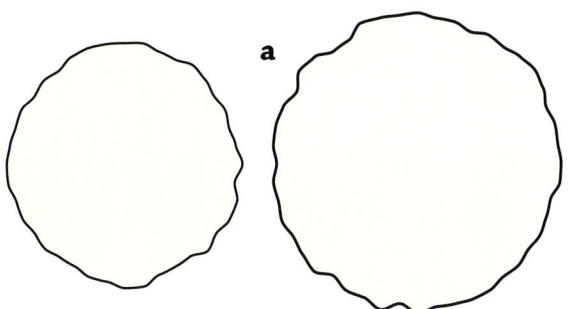

a

2. Follow the steps on page 9 to assemble your design, and to draw in any extra (dotted) lines that were marked on the templates (again, some of these, such as the flower centres, can be done by eye). Lay the backing fabric right side down on a flat surface and position the wadding on top; lay the fused design, right side up, on top so that there's an even border of wadding all the way around the edge of the design. Use your preferred method to secure the layers.

3. Follow the principles on page 4 to 'doodle' round the motifs (**b**), beginning with any shapes that go into or behind others. Once the outsides of all the flowers, leaves and stems have been stitched, doodle round all the flower centres. If you've included alliums, create an explosion of stitched lines coming out from the centre of each flower-head as shown (**c**).

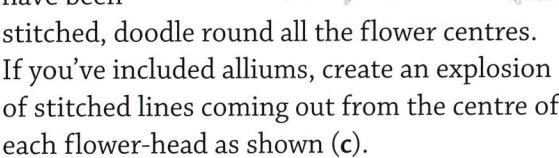

b

c

4. Use a rotary cutter, ruler and board to trim the quilt down to an accurate rectangle, and use the binding strip to add a continuous binding around the raw edges. Add any embellishments (buttons, beads, charms etc) you wish. To hang the quilt, add a hidden casing at the top of the quilt on the back, or stitch on hanging loops of ribbon or tape.

# Show-Stopper Garden

As a spectacular finale to the projects, I've created a cottage garden using most of the flowers featured in the templates! The result is a riot of different colours and textures – great fun.

*Finished size: my example is 24 x 26in (60 x 66cm). As with the tall cottage garden, you need a depth of at least 24in (60cm) if you're going to use hollyhocks, foxgloves or delphiniums, but as always you can alter the dimensions of the quilt as much as you like. Just alter the wadding and backing accordingly (the backing fabric and wadding should be about 2in/5cm larger than the background), and the length of the binding strip.*

**As well as the items on page 4 you will also need:**

- background fabric 24 x 26in (60 x 66cm)
- large scraps of cotton fabrics in a mixture of bright colours for the flowers, and a good selection of greens for the stems and leaves
- backing fabric, 26 x 28in (66 x 72cm)
- 3½yd (3.5m) binding strip that complements or contrasts with your background fabric; I used a single binding cut 2in (5cm) wide
- 1yd (1m) double-sided bonding web, 18in (45cm) wide; if you are creating a larger design, you will need more bonding web
- flat wadding, 26 x 28in (66 x 72cm)

## Instructions

1. From the templates on pages 15-24, choose the plants that you would like to feature on your design. Follow the steps on pages 3 and 9 to trace, fuse and cut out the flowers, and to assemble any hollyhocks, delphiniums or foxgloves. Use a similar method if you are assembling irises, and for individual small blossoms with centres, such the French Marigolds or whole daisy blooms. If you'd like to include alliums in your design, follow the instructions on page 11 to create the flower-heads and stems.

2. Follow the steps on page 9 to assemble your design, and to draw in any extra (dotted) lines that were marked on the templates (again, some of these,

such as the flower centres, can be stitched by eye). Lay the backing fabric right side down on a flat surface and position the wadding on top; lay the fused design, right side up, on top so that there's an even border of wadding all the way around the edge of the design. Use your preferred method to secure the layers.

3. Follow the principles on page 4 to 'doodle' round the motifs, beginning with any shapes that go into or behind others. Once the outsides of all the flowers, leaves and stems, and the leaf veins, have been stitched, doodle round all the flower centres etc. If you've included alliums, create an explosion of stitched lines coming out from the centre of each flower-head as shown in the photographs.

4. Use a rotary cutter, ruler and board to trim the quilt down to an accurate rectangle, and use the binding strip to add a continuous binding around the raw edges. Add any embellishments you wish. To hang the quilt, add a hidden casing at the top of the quilt on the back, or stitch on hanging loops of ribbon or tape.

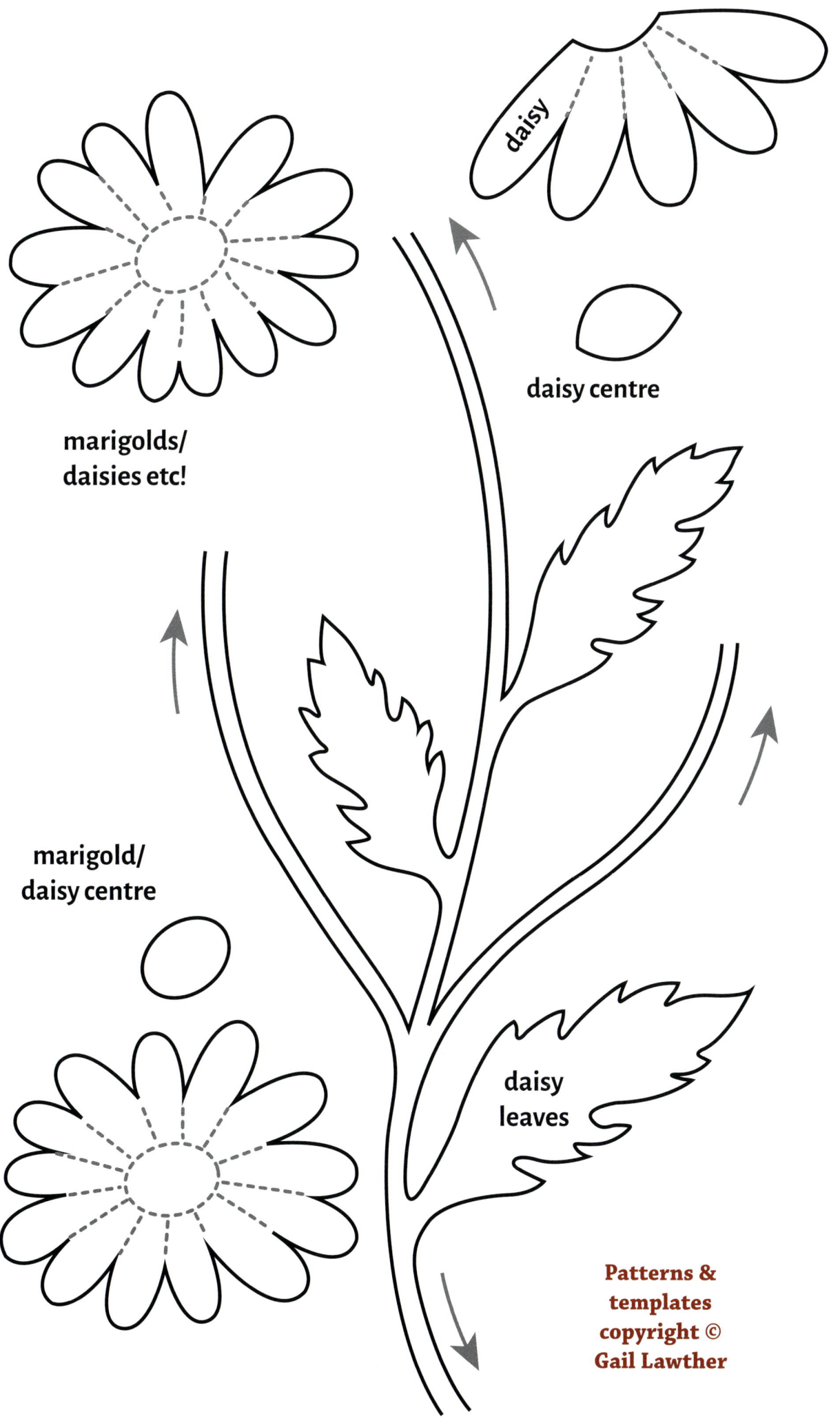

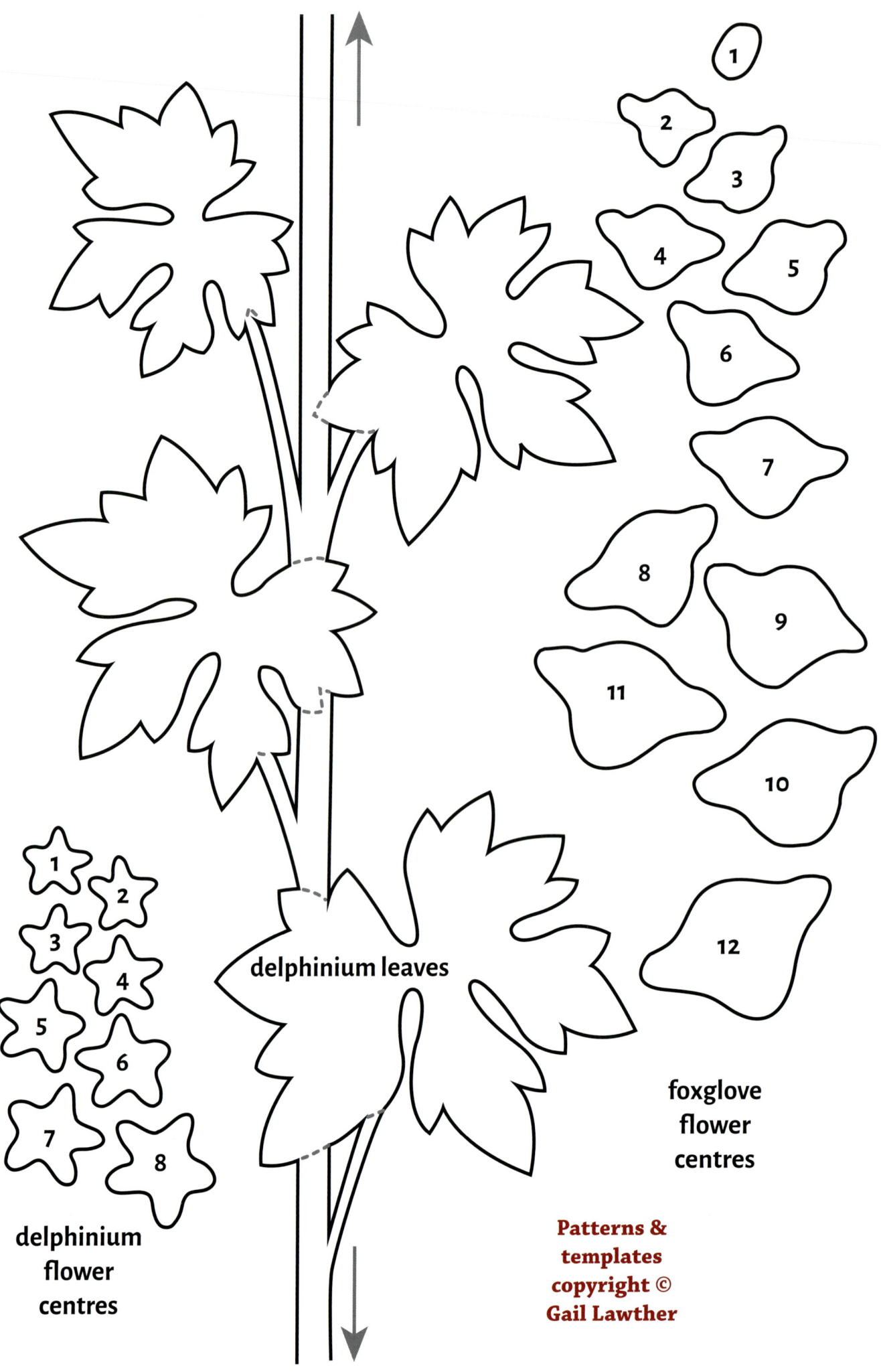

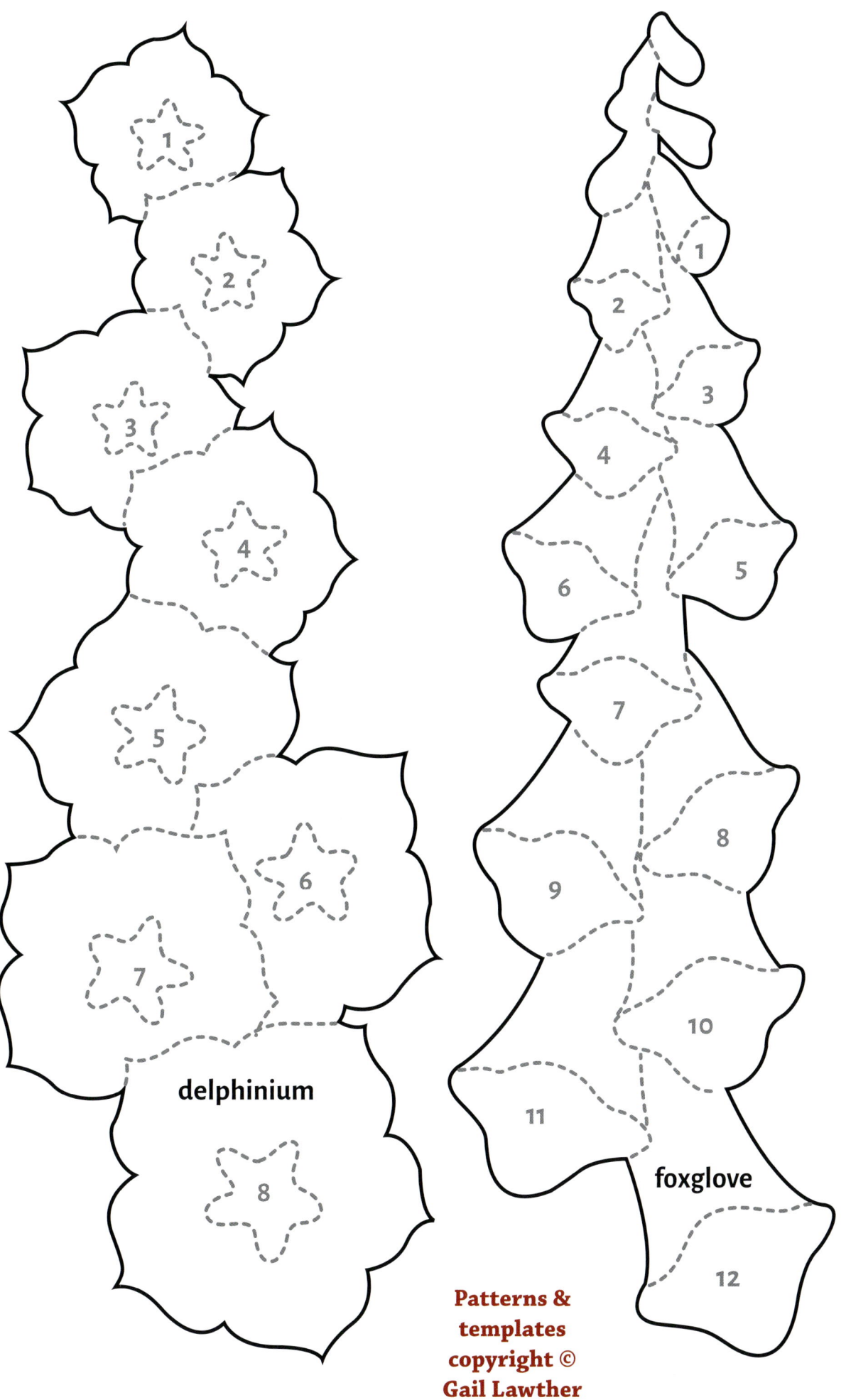

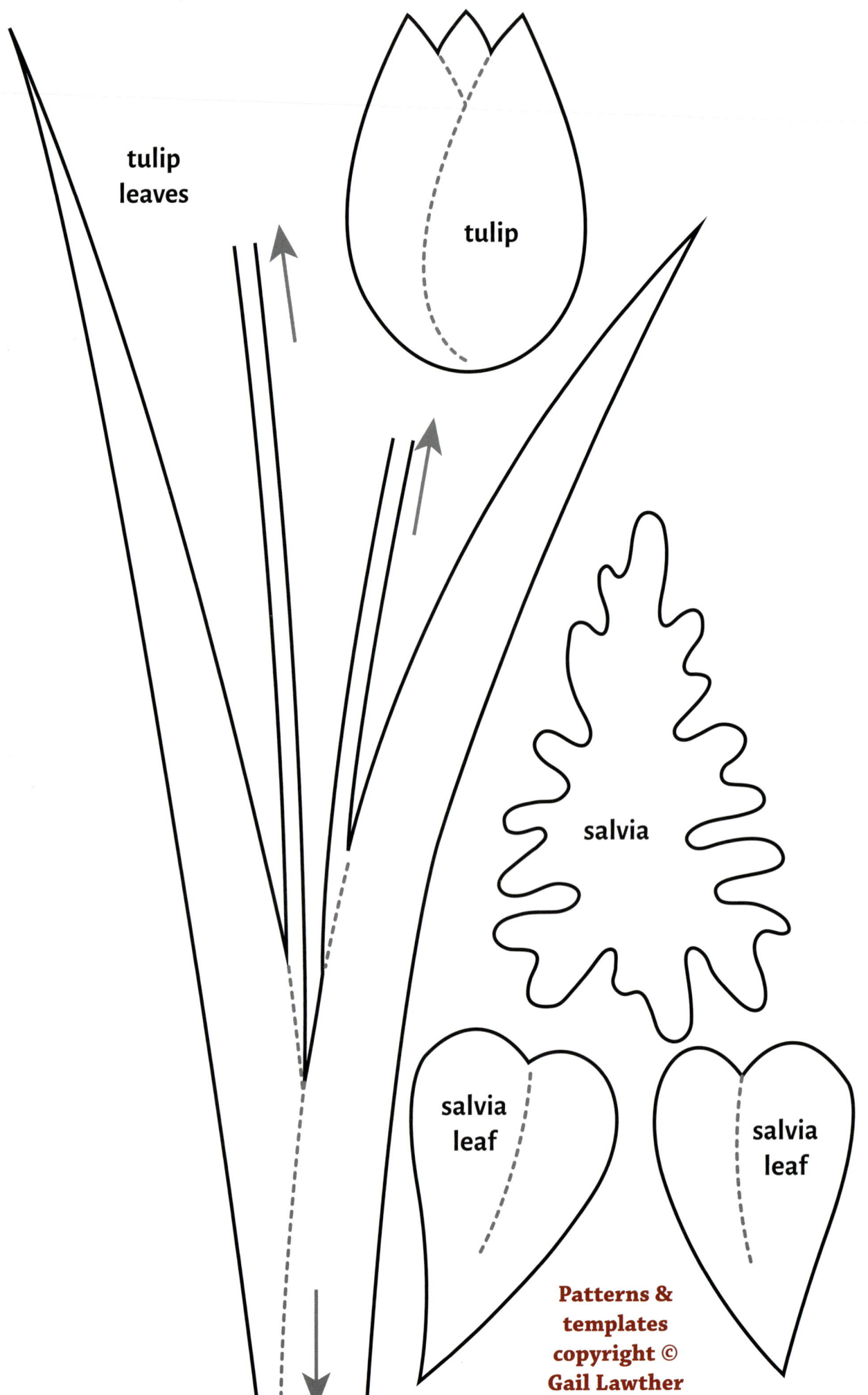

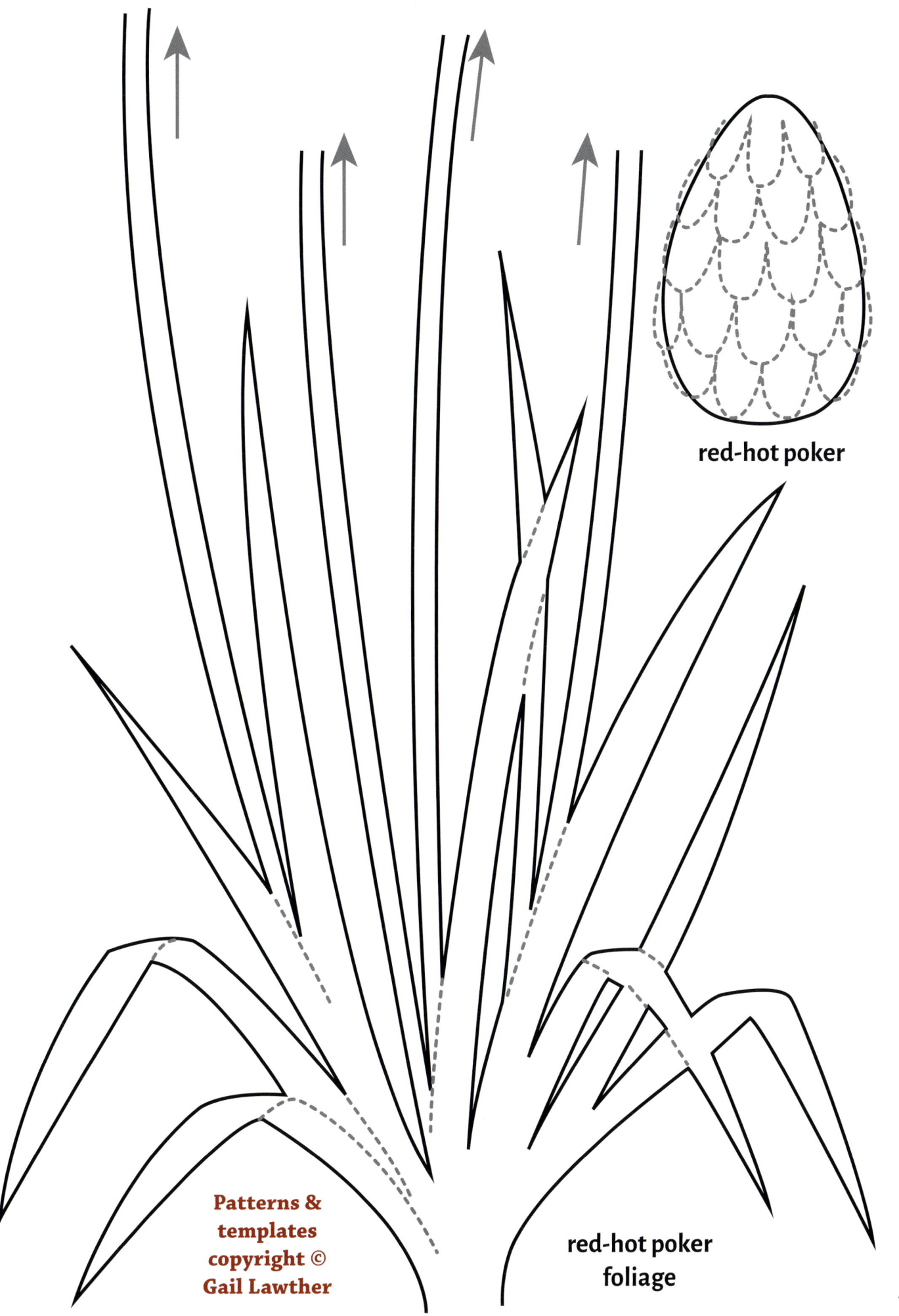

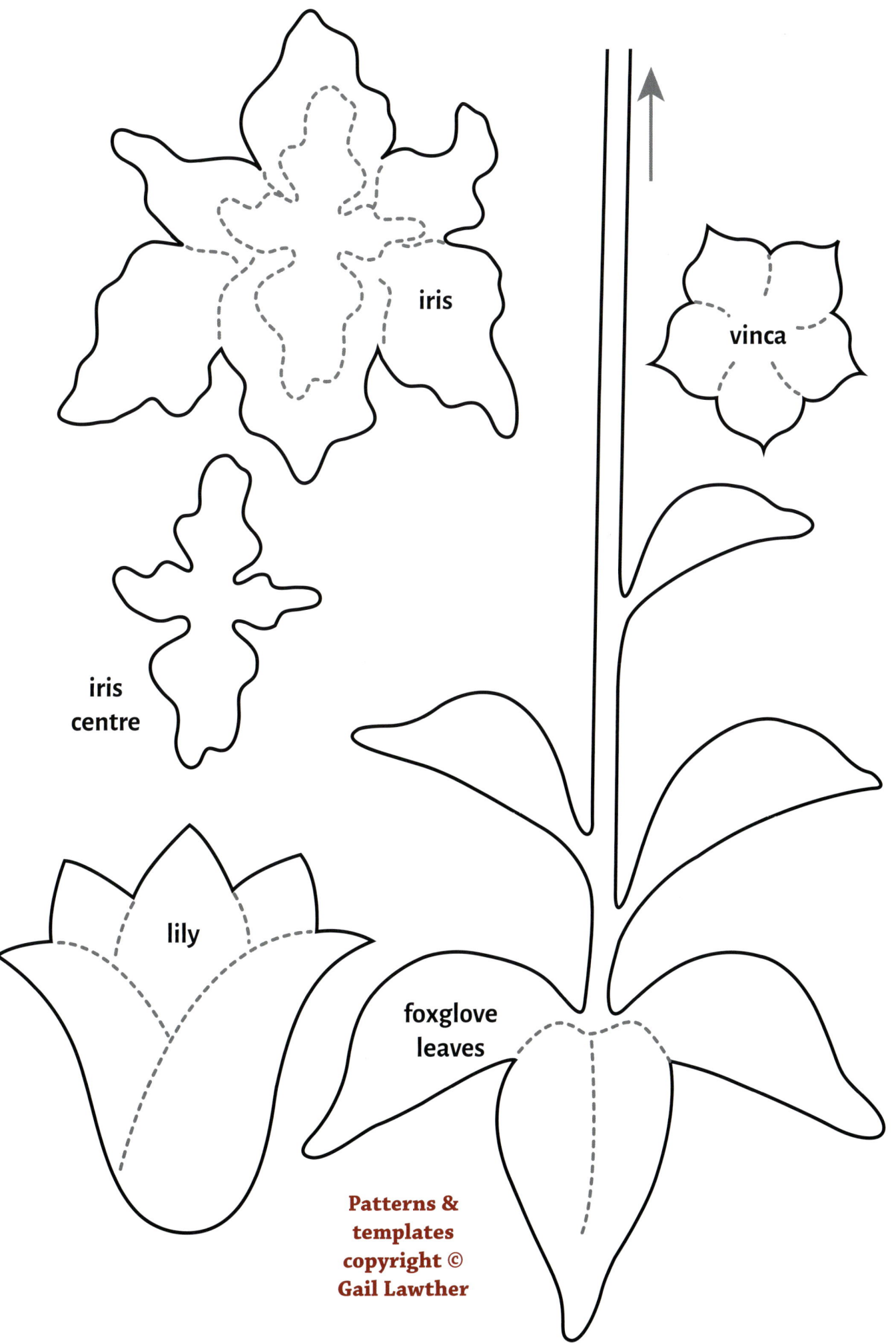

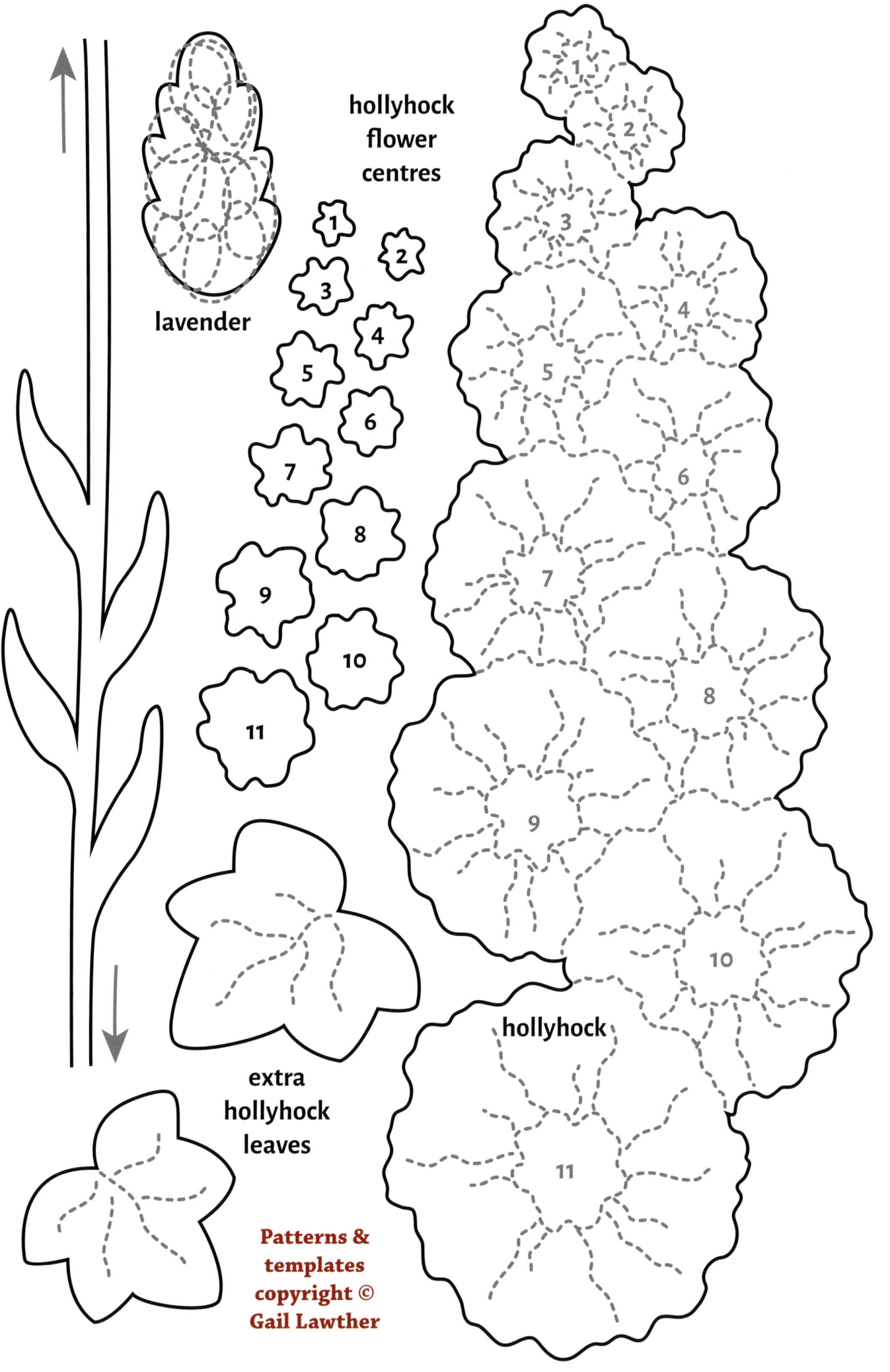

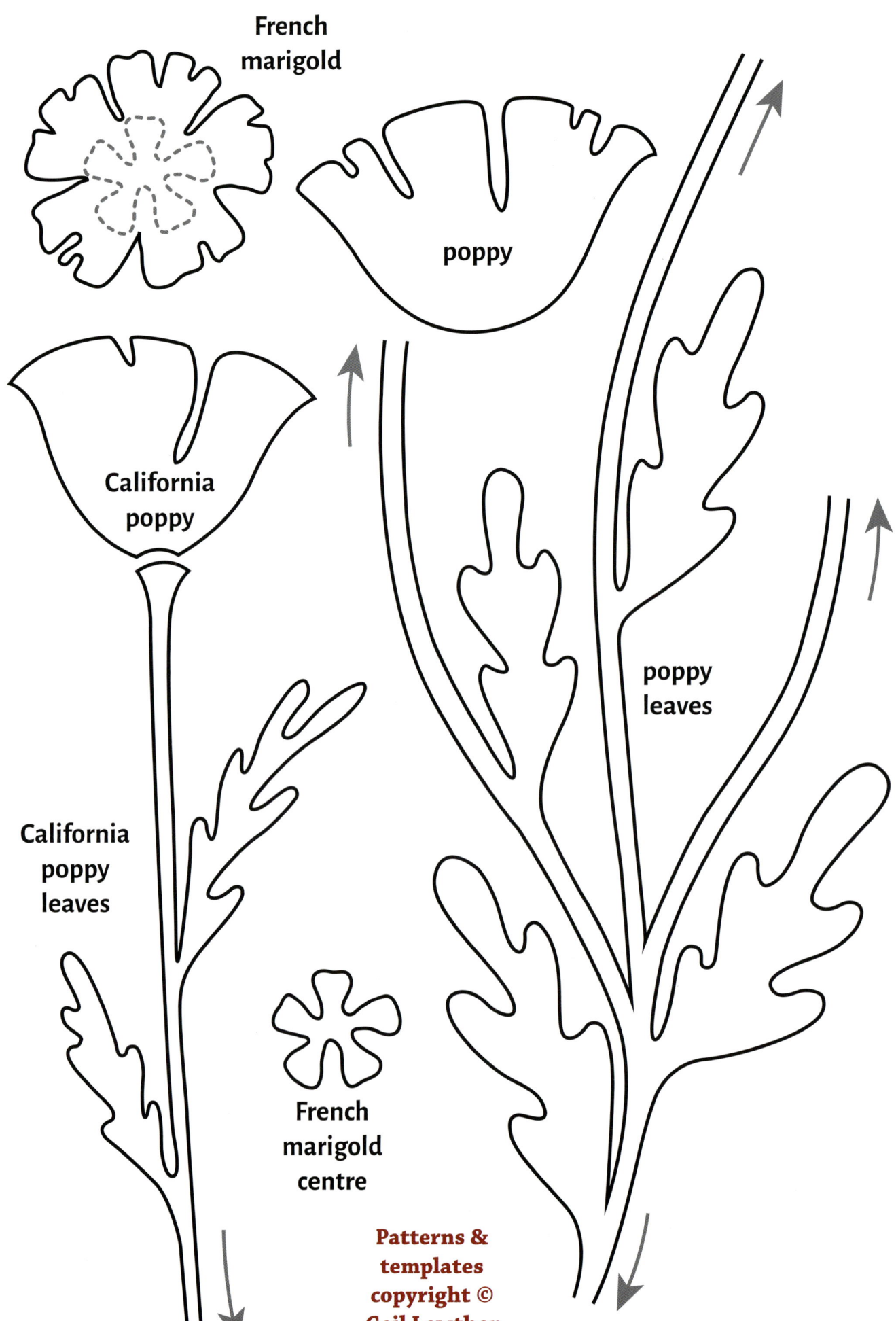